The

Mystery of Man

Professor Hilton Hotema

ISBN: 978-1-63923-124-9

Printed: January 2022

Cover Art By: Paul Amid

Published and Distributed By:
Lushena Books
607 Country Club Drive, Unit E
Bensenville, IL 60106
www.lushenabks.com

ISBN: 978-1-63923-124-9

The Mystery of Man
Professor Hilton Hotema

Table of Contents

Chapter No. 1
Evolution

At the close of the 18th century, modern science was still in utter darkness as to the Mystery of Man. Then in the 19th century came the great evolutionists, Darwin, Wallace, Spencer, Fiske, Huxley, and Haeckel.

A wave of excitement swept over the world. The Mystery of Man has been solved. He is an improved Ape. And for the next half century pseudo-scientists were busy writing books to picture the "progress" of the ape on to the stone-age man, and on to modern man, the scientist.

O.A. Wall, M.D., Ph.G., Ph.M., in his great work, *Sex and Sex Worship,* published in 1918, said:

"I graduated as a physician from Bellevue Medical College in the same year that Darwin published his work on to the 'Descent of Man;' the 'Conflict between Science and Religion' which ensued, was fought out and the truth of the theory of evolution was established within the period of my professional career. And with this victory of human thought, many superstitions faded away" (p. 37).

Time has proven that Wall reached the wrong conclusion. With the origin of man settled, the next step was to solve the problem of his animation. What makes him a living soul?

Then up rose the great Osler, and with haughty ease and mighty wisdom, he filled in this gap by solemnly declaring: "Life is the expression of a series of chemical changes" (Mod. Med. 1907, p. 39). Another great scientist, Alexis Carrel, was not so easily satisfied about the *Mystery of Man.* He said, "The science of man is still too rudimentary to be useful" (*Man The*

Unknown p. 179). That means the complete collapse of the theory of evolution. And we are right back where we began two hundred years ago.

The work of the evolutionists gave the world two theories of existence, which some students describe by the terms Evolution and Involution, and refer respectively to God and to Environment as the source of origin.

Evolution: A series of things unrolled, unfolded, or evolved; as, the evolution of the ages. — Dictionary

Involution: The Action of involving or enfolding; the state of being entangled; complexity; a complication. — Dictionary

The definition of Involution exactly describes the position of the Inductive Scientists. They are so badly entangled in the complexity and complication of their theories of man, that their bewilderment is complete.

A few facts have indeed been verified and recorded by the Inductive Scientists, and a few laws have been approximately formulated. But all of this is subject to revision or even reversion tomorrow. Give to this Science the broadest scope and broadcast scope and most liberal meaning claimed for it, and still it has no existence save in man's imagination. It is no sense stands for Nature, but is, at best, Nature reflected in the beclouded and contradictory Mind of the Inductive Scientist.

Nature presents realities, but the Inductionist deals with shadows and phantoms. Harmonious relation of the varied parts, otherwise termed consistency or congruity, is the acknowledged fact of Universal Existence.

The whole, being composed of the parts, makes every part necessarily consistent with the whole.

The most perfect analogies will be found between the parts.

That is the reason why Nature, true Science, and logic are indissolubly connected, illustrating the same principles and tending to the same conclusions. Not only does every particle of matter in the universe agree with every other particle, process and product, but with these must also agree and be in perfect harmony, every postulate and every conclusion.

To discover the Eternal Unity at the Center where all the parts meet, and the Eternal Plan by which they are all merged into a consistent whole, is to make the basic discovery that solves the Riddle of the Universe. The Leading question is whether the process of transformation is one of evolution or of involution.

Prof. Henry Drummond was enthusiastic about the theory of evolution that swept the world of science in the 19th. Century, and discussed it with much fluency in his "Natural Law in the Spiritual World," but more especially in his "Ascent of Man," concluding the later work with a chapter on Involution, in which he repeats and condenses his arguments of his Natural law, and urges that the supreme factor in all development is Environment."

He said that "tree and root find their explanation not in something in themselves, but mainly in something outside of themselves."

"The secret of Evolution lies," he says, "with Environment." Then, as if to explain his statements more fully, he says: "Evolution is not to unfold from within; it is to unfold from without" (Ascent of Man, p. 324).

The scientists and theorists make their own definition of words to suit their own convenience and notions. Environment cannot produce that which did not previously exist potentially.

But once a thing comes into being, Environment may supply the conditions, or constitute the occasion, for calling forth the powers, not of the Environment, but inherent in the thing itself.

The process is Evolution in its only true sense — the outworking of internal powers. But the evolutionists reverse the process, making it the in working of external forces.

The basic question is, are vital phenomena of all kinds, the product of external agencies, or of internal forces? Is Life the product of food, or a Principle of Existence? Does Life depend upon food, or use it for its purposes?

Herbert Spencer devoted many chapters of his work to the elucidation of theories on which to base a consistent definition of Life. But he failed to begin at the beginning. Like the true Evolutionist, Spencer began with the assumption of the existence of organic matter, but without even suggestion how or where he got it.

After appropriating, without acknowledgement, this product of Life, he then proceeds to show its remarkable instability, which makes it subject to changes under the slightest influences.

Who ever saw corn change to wheat, or apples change to oranges? Or an ape change to a man? But such is the theory of evolution.

Entirely ignoring these facts of nature, Spencer proceeds to suggest, not to prove, that Life is the product of incidental and external forces which, by accident it may be, have come in contact with Matter. He admits that he does not understand nerve force, but asserts that it is 'habitually generated in all animals, save the lowest, by incident forces of every kind." A poor explanation of an unsolved mystery.

If external forces, produces our thoughts, feelings, sense,

ambitions, activities, why should they not produce Life itself? If they can produce the lower manifestations of Life, why not the higher? That is what the evolutionists teach — Life and all that follows are the products of incidental and external forces, emanating from the Environment. In building up his theory of Life, Spencer exhibits much doubt and hesitancy. But the conclusion is finally reached, and the finished product appears in these words:

"The broadest and most complete definition of Life will be — the continuous adjustment of internal relations to external relations."

According to that definition, Life, is simply a name applied to certain processes of change taking place in Matter, as the product of external forces. In short, "Life is a mode of motion."

Spencer does not deny the existence of internal and intrinsic forces; but he considers that Life is unworthy of being constituted of them. "Force," he agrees, '"is the ultimate principle of existence, but Life is not such a force." What is this "force" that "is the ultimate principle of existence"?

He claims that his system is Evolution, but to sustain his claim, he is compelled to make his own dictionary. He said:

"Evolution is an integration of Matter and concomitant, dissipation of Motion, during which the Matter passes from an indefinite, incoherent homogeneity to a definite, coherent heterogeneity, and during which the retained motion undergoes a parallel transformation."

Is all this work subject to any law? Spencer fails to mention any law.

According to modern science, the universe is a product resulting from the "blind dance of atoms," which do what they assumption of a self-existent something that is the Source and Author of all, whether intellectual, animal, vegetable, or divine, must also begin with the existence of a Something that shall answer to all its parts and processes.

It is the discovery of that Something, in our study of the writings of the Ancient Masters, which has enabled us to produce this work.

It is the discovery of that something which has constrained us to attack the theories, and expose the errors, and controvert the conclusions of those who, by every right of position and learning, were our own teachers.

Chapter No. 2
What Is Man

After studying Man for forty years, the great scientist Dr. Alexis Carrel found Man to be a mystery so confusing that he wrote a book, published in 1935, titled *"Man the Unknown,"* in which he flatly declared, "In fact, our ignorance (of Man) is profound" (p.4).

On the very first page of this book, he began with this statement:

"Those who investigate the phenomena of Life are as if lost in an inextricable jungle, in the midst of a magic forest, whose countless trees unceasingly change their place and their shape. These investigators are crushed by a mass of facts which they can describe but are incapable of defining in algebraic equations" (Ibid, p. 1).

In his attempt to describe man, Dr. H.H. Sheldon, University of New York increased the confusion by stating: "We as individuals undoubtedly have no existence in reality, other than as waves, multitudinous and complicated centers, perhaps, in what is called the ether."

As they attempt to describe Man as a physical being, biologists find themselves wandering in Sheldon's "waves."

They discover that man's body is composed of cells, that the cells are composed of molecule, the molecules composed of atoms, the atoms composed of electrons, and the electrons as whirling centers of cosmic force in the ether.

In view of these statements and findings, the big questions are, what is Man? What is Life?

In studying Man for what he seems to be, science is actually studying a Phantasma, an imaginary existence that seems to be real, a Phantom that cannot be pinned down, a will-o-the-wisp that ever dances before us like a rainbow, but always eludes our grasp.

The findings of these scientific investigations show that:

> 1. What we call Life seems to be but a word or name that defines nothing but an appearance, and means only a Conscious Knowledge of our existence and our environment.

> 2. What we call Man seems to be but a word or name applied to Incarnate Spirit appearing on the Visible Plane.

The facts show that what we call Life and Man appear as illusions of the senses; a Phantasma that we think we see, but fades into the invisible realm when we attempt to describe it. It seems that what we call Life, Living, being Alive, are terms which describe a certain Effect on the Mind.

The Late Dr. Robert A. Millikan, world renowned scientist, head of the California Institute of Technology, authority on Cosmic Rays, said:

"I cannot explain why I am alive rather than dead. Physiologists can tell me much about the mechanical and chemical processes of my body, but they cannot say why I am alive" (Collier's, Oct. 24, 1925.)

The mechanical and chemical processes of the living body are evidence of the presence of a mysterious force the nature of which, declare the leading biologists, is unknown.

Man's body appears as a highly organized Unit of vibratory waves. These waves do not radiate at random, but in a fixed and orderly course, and produce conditions and results according to unchangeable law.

The Mystery called Man is only the EFFECT that appears on the visible plane, and that EFFECT has no existence save in the brain of Man as a STATE OF CONSCIOUSNESS.

Of course material science will object to some of these statements, terming them unsound and unscientific. But it is groping in the dark and is unable to define Life and Man in logical terms, or to offer any reasonable evidence to show the foregoing statements are unsound or unscientific.

O, Man, Know They Self

In this the 20th century, with publications and periodicals filled with boasting about the "March of Science," we still have no answers to the most fundamental questions of life.

If we begin with the question, (1) what is Life? Science has no answer.

If we ask (2) is Life Eternal? Science has no answer.

If we ask (3) what is Man? Science has no answer.

In the field where our studies should start, is neglected and left in a mass of talented vines and brush. The reason is that modern science is mercialistic and not humanistic. It is interested in moneymaking inventions and not in Man's betterment.

Alipilli, an advanced philosopher of the mystic school of Alexandria, said:

"The universal orb or the world contains not so great mysteries and excellences as man •••. He who desires the primacy among the students Of nature, will nowhere find a greater field of study than himself. So, with a loud voice I proclaim, O, Man, Know Thy Self"

(Solar logos, p. 27).

The greatest mysteries of the universe are those by which we are surrounded; so trite and common that we never reflect on them.

Scientists tell us of the laws that regulate the motions of the planets; of centripetal and centrifugal forces, gravity and attraction, electricity and magnetism, and all the other high-sounding terms invented to hide a want of meaning. These scientists but hide their ignorance in a cloud of words, and the words too often are mere combinations of sounds without meaning. What is centrifugal force? A tendency to go in a particular direction. What is the other force, then which produces that tendency?

What force draws the needle round to the north? What force moves muscles and raises the arm, when the will determines it shall rise? Or moves the leg, or makes the heart beat?

These are miracles; inexplicable as the creation, or the existence of Polarized Atoms.

What mystery are the effects of heat and cold on water. What mystery is hidden in the snow flake, in every crystal of ice, in their final transformation into invisible vapor that rises land and sea and floats above the mountain tops?

Who will explain the passion, peevishness, anger, memory, affections? The conscious of identity and the dreams of man? The modes of communication of thoughts of the ant and bee?

Who has yet made us to understand how the image of external objects fix themselves upon the retina of the eye; and when there, how the mere empty, unsubstantial image becomes transmuted into the wondrous phenomenon called Sight? Or who the waves of the air, striking upon the tympanum of the ear, produce the wondrous phenomenon of Hearing?

Our senses are mysteries to us, and we are mysteries to ourselves. Philosophy has taught us nothing but words as to the nature of our sensation, perceptions, our cognizance's, the origin of our thoughts and ideas.

By no effort nor degree of reflection, no matter how long continued, can man become conscious of a personal identity in himself separate and distinct from his body and brain.

Who has yet made us to understand how, from the contact with a foreign body, the image in the eye, the wave of air impinging on the ear, particular particles entering the nostrils, or coming in contact with the palate, cause sensations in the nerves, and from that perception in the mind.

What do we know of Substance? Scientists even doubt whether it" exists. Prof. Sheldon declares that "We as individuals have no existence in reality, other than as waves, — multitudinous and complicated centers in what is called the ether."

The noted astronomer, Sir James Jeans, says, "All the choir of heaven and all the furniture of earth have no existence outside of Mind."

Philosophers tell us that our senses only make known to us

the attributes of substance, but not the thing itself. We knew the attributes of the Soul, its thoughts and perceptions, but what do we know of the Soul itself that which perceives and thinks? How can we, with our limited mental vision, expect to grasp and comprehend the mysteries of the Great Universe?

Infinite Space, extending from us in every direction, without limit; infinite Time without beginning or end; and we, here and now, in the center of each. Our earth, spinning upon its axis, and rushing ever in its circuit round the Sun; and our Sun and all our solar system, revolving round some other great central point.

Our Sun, the center of its own system, and this system the center of a larger system, and on to incomparably larger systems, until we reach what must be the Supreme Center of all.

Such are some of the mysteries of the Grand Universe, the answers to which science cannot give us.

Chapter No. 3
World of Illusion

"The world is a fleeting show, for man's illusion given." — Moore.

When Moore penned that passage he must have had in mind the scientists of the last three centuries, who thought the earth was flat and stationary, assumed the Universe to be a dead machine, and believed in the absolute void of celestial space.

Until quite recently, the "scientists" of the 20th century follow the same path, filling their text-books with plausible theories of Materialism and Evolutionism. The fundamental dogma of physical science declared that "All is physical matter and mechanical energy." They had solved the riddle of the Universe.

With its major premise exploded by the discovery that solid Matter is an illusion, physical science is now engaged in twisting and distorting recent findings in an effort to "save face" **by** trying to make these findings fit and support the crumbling theories and absurd conclusions with which its text-books are filled,

These "great scientists" had scornfully ridiculed the suggestion of a Spiritual World as ancient superstition. Recent discoveries show that so-called solid Matter is nothing more than Spiritual Substance in condensed form.

Spirit and Matter are new found to be two aspects of **the** same thing, the one condensed and visible, called Matter, the other gaseous and invisible, called Spirit. Yet both are identical in their elemental nature.The "absolute void of celestial space" postulated **by** physical science, is found to be filled with wonders that are as staggering as they are startling. The

14

discovery of these wonders of the Spiritual World has only begun in modern times. It is asserted by some thinkers that the discovery of the Angelic Department of the Universe, so vehemently scorned by physical science, may not be far off.

According to late discoveries, several degrees of Spirit exist, to-wit:

1. Spirit as solid, liquid and gaseous states.
2. Spirit as rarefied gases, consisting of separate molecules, and molecules resolved into component atoms.
3. Spirit as radiant force--light, electricity, magneticity, etc.

This is turned the electronic state of Matter, or electrons with their derivatives not combined into atoms. The theory of two worlds, one spiritual and the other physical is based on the principle of Dualism, and arises from appearance. Unity and Universe mean One World, not two.

In this Universe of Change, the scientists are deceived by the Pairs of Opposites that incessantly appear as the orderly work of the Transformative Process.

The Masters, rising above the Plane of Dualism, visualized one world with Dual Aspects.

The Plane of Dualism is the Plane of Illusion. Our senses, through their faculties of the Mind, give us reports of changes occurring in the Realm of Dualism, where the Sun seems to rise and set, and man seems to come in birth and go in death. These changes are shifting and impermanent, transient and inconstant.

Volumes have been written about Two Worlds, and the present and the future life. Between these two is assumed to be a void, a gulf impassable except through the portals of Death.

As there is One World with two aspects, so there is One Life with.

Under the Law of Cycles, the Wheels of Transformation constantly turn. In their orderly revolution they present two aspects of the Unit. The invisible portion is termed the Spiritual World, while the visible portion is called the Physical World. Physical science would now like to forget all that its text books contain, consisting of empty theories built on assumptions that the Universe was a dead machine, and celestial space was absolutely void.

It now appears that "a tiny whirling, invisible speck, considered pure electricity, is the basis of all familiar Matter" (Electronics). Millikan declares that "Electrons are the building blocks of the Universe." The Universe is composed of electrons, which are "electronic spiritual substance, the first form that Spirit assumes as Matter". The transition of Spirit to Matter, and Matter to Spirit, is now an established fact.

Atoms are transformed into radiation, as in radio-activity, and radiation into Matter, as protons of gamma rays. This discovery also establishes the surprising fact that recreation" is a process of condensation of Spiritual Substance, and its transformation into physical forms according to 'intelligence and law that appear to be inherent in Spiritual Substance.

'This new understanding of Spirit and Matter is the greatest miracle of modern times. It enables us to understand scientifically the spiritual origin of all visible things, including Man. Ancient scriptures contain evidence to show that the Ancient Masters understood those things.

The smallest portion of the elements that may not be further divisible without changing its characteristics, is the atom, which consists of electrons revolving in one or more separate orbits around one or more centrally located nuclei, and held in that orbit, and in its motion around that orbit, by centripetal .and centrifugal force, acting together intelligently and according to law.

Intelligence is not confined to the brain, as we find these elements rigidly obeying law, and that is more than the possessor of brains usually do.

The motion of the electron requires force, which it appears to receive from the cosmic source; and that force, in turn, is emitted by or radiated from the atom. It is this power that animates the cells of the human body, and is termed vital force, brain force, nerve force, etc.., deriving its name from the organ in which it appears.

The atom consists of only one element, divided to the component where it ceases to be that element if further charged.

When the atoms of two or more elements are added together they form an entirely different material from the original element of which composed; and when the new material is divided until the smallest portion of it is obtained where it would be different if further divided, that smallest amount is known as a molecule of that particular combination.

Most of the more common combinations of atoms have names. Thus, water consists of 3 atoms, 2 elements of hydrogen and one of oxygen. When the 3 atoms are combined in the proper manner, they form a molecule of an entirely different material, with characteristics different from either of the elements of which it is composed.

This combining of elements continues still further, when molecules of different elemental combinations are themselves joined. They then form more complex combinations that are different from anything else composed of identically the same molecules. Examples of this are the various kinds of tissues and organs in the body. It is not known how electrons become combined into atoms, just as it is not known how molecules become combined into cells and protoplasm to build and sustain the living body. But it has become apparent that the body is not built by food. It seems that food is the occasion and condition that activates the vital processes and stimulates their activity.

The transformation of visible matter to invisible substance is the reverse process. The change of matter from solid to liquid and to gaseous substance concerns molecules only, i.e., the distance between them and their cohesion. The atoms do not change.

Within the molecule, in all three states of matter (solid, liquid gaseous), everything remains the same, i.e., the proportion of matter to emptiness does not alter. Electrons remain equally far from one another inside the atom, and revolve in their orbits in the same way in all states of cohesion of the molecule. Changes in the density of matter, i.e., transition from solid into liquid and gaseous states, do not in any way affect the electrons.

The world inside the molecule is exactly analogous to the great space in which the celestial bodies move. which space scientists believed to be void and empty. Electrons, atoms, molecules, planets, solar systems, agglomerations of stars — all these are phenomena of the same order.

Electrons move in their orbits in the atom in the cells of the human body, just as planets move in their orbit in the solar systems of the Universe. The power of movement cares not from food.

The electrons in the atoms in the cells of the human body are the same celestial bodies as the planets of the sky. Even their voicoity is the same.

This fact means that the human body resembles the planetary bodies. The Ancient Masters said, "As above, so below." Man is microcosm and the Universe is microcosm.

If the planetary bodies depend not on food for their origin and maintenance, why should the human body? The law never changes.

In the world of electrons and atoms, it is possible to observe all the phenomena that are observed in the astronomical world. There are comets in the atom that travel from one system to another; there are shooting stars; there are streams of meteorites.

"As above so below." Physical science must at least admit the truth of the ancient formulas the Ancient Masters, now termed superstitious heathens. But it will be another century before it does so. The substance of which all visible objects consist, including the human body, is constructed in exactly the same way as the solar system. For each atom in the cells of the body is a miniature solar system.

We are incapable of perceiving electrons and atoms as immovable points, but perceive them in the form of the complex, and entangled traces or lines of their movements, which produce the illusion of mass.

Could we perceive our great solar system on an infinitely smaller scale, it would produce on our senses the illusion of a mass of matter. There would be, for us, no emptiness nor space, just as there appears to be no emptiness nor space in Matter surrounding us.

The entire Universe, consisting of innumerable sums and

their surrounding planets, rushing with terrific speed through space, but separated from us by vast distances, is perceived by us as an immovable point.

Our Sun is a star, and, with its attendant planets, is rushing through space at a speed of 200 miles a second, travelling around the center of its cosmic system, ruled by the Law of Polarity.

Electrons, as they move, are transformed into apparent lines, like an object swung round and round with such speed as to form an apparent circle. The apparent lines, intertwining along themselves, produce the illusion of mass, i.e., of solid, impenetrable matter, of which consist the three dimensional bodies surrounding us, including our own organism, a mass of atoms vibrating so swiftly as to appear to be a solid.

What appears as solid matter is an illusion created by speed that appears to form the fine web of lines made by the traces of motion of the smallest material points. An apparently solid bar of steel is as "empty" to certain radiations as is the solar system to our eyes. This fact was demonstrated at the University of Michigan in determining the extent of flaws in metal. By using a tube carrying 250,000 volts, photographs were taken through four inches of apparently solid steel.

The illusive impression of solid matter is produced by the speed of movement. When these principles are mown, we have a conception of the way the web, created by the motion of electrons, is woven and thickened, and have the whole world of infinite variety of phenomena, is constructed from this web of lines, which are made by the traces of the motion of the smallest material points. The sun, moon, stars, which we think we see, we do not see. What we see are only cross-sections of spirals, — a cross section of the web of lines made by the traces of the motion of the smallest material points.

Mass is an illusion and appears as the result of terrific speed of invisible points. A ray of light is substance; so is electric current.

Light and electricity are substance not formed into atoms, but remaining in the electronic state. One author terms electricity "ions in transit."

Man's relation to the universe is fixed by the fact that his body is constituted of a mass of vibrating atoms, combined in form by the law of Polarity.

When Vital Force ceases to operate through the body, the atoms lose their cohesive properties, and the body disintegrates and returns to the original cosmic elements. When something occurs to obstruct the current of Vital Force, somatic death is the result.

A scientist is he who can explain results and the cause that produces them. He must attain to the Principle, which consists of the Force that produces, and the Law that directs the work.

The philosopher who trusts to observation for his facts, is looking at the wrong side of nature. He lives in the World of Illusion, but knows it not. The great truths which have shaken society to its center, have always appeared insignificant to the superficial observer, while to the discoverer, the scientific observer, the comprehensive thinker, tile True Principle is a Pearl of priceless value.

To him who has attained the true vantage-ground by discovering the Principle, mystery fades, speculation gives way to knowledge, and empiricism to the certainty of science.

It was not a lack of facts of observation that prevented the discovery of the circulation of the blood in modern times, nor that left astronomical discoveries of modern times to Copernicus, Kepler, Newton. So it is not a lack of biological, psychological, and physiological facts that prevent the establishment of a Science of Man, or a true philosophy of existence. It is the deliberate work of material science, which stubbornly refuses to recognize the existence of the Spiritual World and Spiritual Man.

It is the Real World, the Spiritual World, the mysterious causes of things, the invisible forces and the laws of their operation, which we must discover if we would know the secrets back of Life and Death.

Chapter No. 4
Cosmic Thought

"Every cosmogony, from the earliest to the latest, is based upon, interlinked with, and most closely related to, numerals and geometrical figures." — Blavatsky, *Secret Doctrine*, 111, 69.

"So teach us to number our days, that we may apply our hearts unto wisdom. "--Ps. xc. 12.

Mathematics is the only exact science — the only one with propositions that are capable of positive proof and conclusive demonstration. All other so-called exact sciences are based assumptions, deductions, inductions and "working hypotheses," which are more or less useful until further investigation and discovery prove them to be but partial truths.

Words are symbols of ideas, but numbers are symbols of Divine Realities, Spiritual Verities eternal in time, which periodically express themselves in the worlds of objectivity.

The Ancient Masters said, "The world is built upon the power of numbers, and numbers are the Key to an understanding of the world."

Numbers are the Key to the ancient views on cosmogony, in its broad sense, including man and beings, and the development of humanity, spiritually as well as physically.

"Hence we find numbers and figures used as an expression and a record of Thought in every archaic symbolical scripture. They ever the same, with certain variations only, arising from the first figures." — Blavatsky, *Secret Doctrine* 1, 341.

The Ancient Masters asserted that the doctrine of Numbers, the chief of all in Esoterism, was revealed to man by the celestial Deities; that the World was produced under the Law of Sound or

Harmony, and according to the principles of musical proportion.

The science of numbers was not slowly developed by primitive man's learning to count on his fingers, as modern science claims in its "face-saving-propaganda."

It was a fully and completely elaborated system of scientific computation, as clearly shown by the Great Pyramid of Egypt, built more than fifty thousand years ago, and containing a perfect system of stone symbols, figures and geometrical commensuration that reveal, through measurements, the mysteries of the Universe.

A system so far ahead of anything that has yet been produced by modern engineers, that the modern world has nothing which can begin to compare with it.

Littlefield holds that this system was revealed to the Ancient Masters by "tutelary spirits; who kept their human students under constant guard." (Way of Life, p. 2l).

The mathematical physicists who have become mathematical metaphysicians, consider the Universe a mathematical structure that is the product and expression of Pure Thought, closely related to, if not identical with, Mind.

Their doctrine of relativity enables them to reach such views as give them a less static and more fluidic Universe, that is more the product of subjective interpretation, than the old mechanistic Universe postulated by physical science.

These metaphysicians have views of the Cosmos that are strongly idealistic, and their conception of the phenomenal world is that it is a symbol of Ultimate Reality — and that Reality is Mind.

Eddington says, "Force and dimensions belong to the world of symbols, and from such conceptions we have built the extern world of physics. After exhausting all physical methods without success, we then returned to the inmost recesses of Consciousness, to the great 'I am Consciousness,' to the Voice that proclaims our Personality, and from there we entered upon a new outlook.

"We must build a Spiritual World out of Symbols, as the Ancient Masters did, such symbols being taken from our own Personality, and we build the scientific world out of the symbols of the mathematician" (*Science & The Unseen World*).

Sir James Jeans, in his Mysterious Universe, quotes Berkeley's statement, which embodies the fundamental idea of his idealistic philosophy, that "all the choir of heaven and all the furniture of earth have no existence without Mind."

He adds, "It matters not whether subjects exist in my Mind, or in that of any other spirit; their objectivity arises from their subsisting in the Mind of sore Eternal Spirit. The Universe can best be pictured, although still imperfectly, as consisting of pure thought. If the Universe is one of Thought, then its production must have been an act of Thought."

'There is a deep, cosmic meaning back of the statement, "For as he thinketh in his heart, so is he" (Ps. 23: 7).

For sixteen centuries darkness has reigned because Romanism, in the 4th century, personified the symbols of the Ancient Masters, which symbols represent Universal Principles, and then distorted and literalized the ancient scriptures, which originally told the true story Allegorically. The entire Universe and all its parts, whether suns, stars, planets, mountains or men, are reducible in the finale to one simple science of vibratory waves that affect our consciousness through our physical senses.

What is Consciousness? That is just another question of

many, modern science cannot answer.

According to the dictionary, Consciousness is: "The knowledge of sensations and mental operations, or of what passes in one's own mind."

Behaviorism declares that man has no consciousness. That statement could possibly be correct. Some authorities hold that the consciousness man appears to have and express, is really the consciousness of God acting upon and through the brain, but limited by capacity of the brain. The Masters taught that the things we think we hear, see, smell, feel and taste, have no actual existence other than as ways forms recognized by our consciousness, which is only an emanation of the great "I AM CONSCIOUSNESS."

Chapter No. 5
Spiritual World (A)

From the dawn of man there seems to have been a firm belief in the existence of a world that cannot be reached nor recognized by the physical senses and faculties.

No tribe of people has been too low in the scale of intelligence to entertain such a belief; and no race of men has been too high in the development of intelligence to reject it.

This fact constrains scholars to believe that such a word must exist; for they contend that man cannot even conceive of anything that is not nor cannot be.

It is a self-evident truth that any conviction which sways the entire human race, regardless of rank or quality, is inherent. It could not be otherwise. There is a universal conviction that man, in the case of somatic dissolution, continues to live spiritually. Then that is one self-evident truth.

This conviction inheres in the Soul and rises from Spiritual Intuition. There is not one instance of record that spiritual Intuition has ever borne false testimony. Nor has it ever deceived or misled any creature. It is also a fact of observation that the lower in the scale of individual intelligence is the creature, the more potent and vital is the intuition that guides it. It is a paradox that the cosmic guiding power appears to be stronger in the more natural and less educated people. What is termed "education" appears to lead people from the natural to the artificial.

Early man appears to have lived a natural life, and was taught by Spiritual Intuition that somatic death is not the end of him. This theory is being confirmed by the best scientific analysis of known facts. Modern man has searched for the

Spiritual World up in the cold spaces intervening in the sky. He has been taught by the church that up there is the Kingdom of Heaven, where God sits on his throne and the gospel Jesus sits on his right hand, Also, that man must be "born of water and of the spirit" before he can inter into that Kingdom (Jn. 3: 5).

From the records that Romanism has permitted to reach the people, it appears that man has been unable to discover the kingdom of Immortal Souls, and that has led him to doubt that there is such a realm, or anything more than that he sees on the physical plane. The result of this is that people are rapidly losing faith in the church, and are leaving it annually by the thousands.

Physical science has made certain important discoveries, to-wit:

1. All matter is reducible to vibratory force.

2. Every particle of matter is in a state of constant vibration.

3. Coarse particles vibrate much more slowly than fine ones.

All visible matter is in a certain stage of refinement and is vibrating at a corresponding rate of degree, as it is termed.

The visible world is composed of substance, and this substance may be reduced to an invisible state. The spiritual part of man is as truly substance as is the physical part, in which the spiritual dwells. Both are substance, and both are in a state of vibration. The physical portion is visible because of its slower vibratory rate. The spiritual portion is invisible because of its faster vibratory rate. This is the conclusion of science.

If it be admitted that the physical and spiritual worlds are composed of substance, the question arises, wherein lies the difference? The one belongs to the realm of purely physical things, and is designated by the very appropriate term physical substance. The one belongs to the realm of purely spiritual things, and is designated by .the equally fitting term spiritual substance.

For a similar reason, we designate that which belongs to the mineral kingdom as mineral, and that which belongs to the vegetable kingdom as vegetable. According to occult science, the difference between physical substance and spiritual substance lies in the rate of vibration.

If we examine a rock, we can discover no vibratory movement. The vibratory motion of the atom in the rock is at such a low rate it is not perceptible to the physical sense of sight, and the rock appears to be a solid, immovable, impenetrable mass of dead matter.

If we examine growing wood in a tree, we are unable to observe any movement among the atoms of which the wood is composed. But if we use a powerful magnifying glass we will be able to detect a slight vibratory motion among the cells of the wood. While the rate of this vibratory motion is much greater than that in the case of the rock, it is still too slow to affect the physical sense of vision. So the wood, like the rock, appears to the naked eye as a solid, dead mass.

To save time and space, we shall pass over the several intermediate substances, such as animal flesh, gelatin, etc., and examine a drop of water. Here the vibratory motion of the atom in the compound is at a rate many times greater than in either rock or wood.

The molecules of which water is composed move with much facility and rapidity, one upon another, that to a certain extent they elude the physical sense of sight, and the result is that water is transparent to the naked eye.

When we come to the gases, the vibratory motion of the atom in the compound is at a rate so much higher, that the physical sense of vision is entirely eluded. Gas is substance that is invisible only because the atoms of which it is composed vibrate so fast that the physical sense of sight is unable to follow them.

When a gun is discharged, we are unable to see the bullet speeding on its way, because the rate of movement is so rapid that the physical sense of sight cannot follow it. It simply eludes the eye.

When a carriage wheel is at rest, we can see every spoke clearly. But place the wheel on a spindle and set it to revolving rapidly, and the faster the rate the less distinctly will we be able to see the spokes, until the spokes finally disappear as the rate of revolution increases.

When we come to electricity, the highest grade of substance known we find that the vibratory motion of the elements in this compound is at a rate higher than that in any other physical world of substance and the spiritual world of substance. The only difference is that we have approached from an entirely different direction, viz., along the line of vibration motion. The next step takes us beyond the physical and into the world of spiritual substance.

The physical scientist, or physicist, using only physical means, is limited in his investigation and demonstration to the world of visible substance, termed. He halts at the border-line between the two worlds of substance, and is forced to say: I can go no further; the instruments at my command are not fine enough, nor sufficiently subtle, to test the properties and qualities of that which lies beyond. It eludes the methods of physical science and all the means at my command.

That is not all. The ethics of physical science forbids scientists to explore the spiritual world under that definition. Physical science has gone on record as declaring that there is no spiritual world, and that ends and closes the question.

The Master, the spiritual scientist, now takes up the thread, and follows it forward past the border-line of physics into the realm of Psychics. In the Master's ability thus to view the subject of both worlds, and the two aspects of One World, his great advantage is inconceivable to one whose sense of vision and investigation is limited to the world of purely physical things.

At the border-line between the two aspects of substance, the Master sees every law of physical substance joined to its correlative law of spiritual substance. The chain of cosmic law is thus continuous and unbroken. It runs from the visible aspect of the Cosmos directly on to the invisible aspect without interruption.

In this splendid continuity, the Master recognizes the majesty, the power and the glory in the Universality of Law.

Chapter No. 6
Spiritual World (B)

We have noticed briefly the Law of Vibration and the infinity of substance.

We learn that man has a natural or physical body, and in all ages the poets have sung of the spiritual body (1 Cor, 15: 44). These bodies, two in one, are controlled, directed and operated by the Divine Entity, the Intelligent Ego.

This is another example of the Eternal Trinity, met with on every plane of existence.

Adopting this basic premise as our working principle, we proceed to consider the purely rational and scientific means and methods of the Masters. The law we evoke to carry out our demonstration is the Law of Vibration — that Cosmic Law which refines substance and intensifies its action.

The infinite particles of which the body is composed, are collected, collated, correlated, condensed and consolidated into flesh, then move at a correspondingly low rate of vibratory action.

The body is provided with physical sensory organs through which the Spiritual Man contacts his physical environment. The power back of these organs is actually spiritual, proven by the fact that the eye of an unconscious man sees nothing. These organs are not adapted to the rapid vibrations of spiritual substance, nor to all vibrations of physical substance. Their combined powers embrace only a limited range of vibration.

This limited range includes only the vibrations of physical substance which lies and exists upon the same plane of refinement and vibratory action as the physical body itself.

Furthermore, our language has been developed to correspond with that degree of refinement and vibratory action. That is the reason why it is so difficult to describe things spiritual in words of a language evolved to describe only the physical.

By the aid of our physical sensory organs, we become cognizant of different external physical objects, elements and conditions. Beyond this, we know nothing of the universe, the major part of which must remain unknown to us; and our recognition of that concerning which we have conscious knowledge, constitutes what we term physical sensation, which is really a spiritual function. Each one of the physical organs of sensation receives and registers a different range of vibrations. The whole surface of the physical body is supplied with sensory nerves, so as to be and become a medium of vibrations.

The general sense of touch is experienced when any portion of the physical body contacts physical substance that is composed of the coarser particles moving at the lower rates of vibrations. The physical eye is a highly specialized organ of physical sensation. When the eye is brought in contact with rays of physical light, which rays are only fine particles of physical substance moving at a high rate of vibration, we experience the sensation of sight.

As with the eye, so with the ear. When the physical organs of hearing are touched by physical atmosphere moving at certain rates of vibration, the person hears physical sounds.

As with the ear, so with the special physical organs of smell and taste. Both of these organs represent still other and different rates of vibration that obtain in external substance.

Every physical organ of sensation is an organ of touch or contact. The general sense of touch that obtains upon the entire surface of the physical body differs from physical sight only in degree. The one registers the slow vibrations of coarse material particles, while the other registers the rapid vibrations of finer material particles.

Through the operations of these several physical organs, each registering a different range of vibration, the Intelligent Ego comes into conscious relations with a wide range of vibratory activity of physical substance.

The physical sensory organs and the physical brain are constituted and adapted to receive and register only the vibrations of what we term physical substance. They are adapted to receive only a limited range of physical vibrations. This fact is proven by physical science.

For example, the animalcule that swarm upon the earth, in air, water, and in all living bodies, are intangible and invisible to the physical sensory organs. They affect neither the sense of touch nor of hearing, taste, smell nor sight. Except for the microscope, physical science would declare that a belief in animalcule were a superstition.

X-ray makes no impression upon the highest physical organ of sensation, but the x-ray is a vibration of physical substance.

When we realize the marked limitations of the physical senses in a physical world, it is easy to understand why these organs fail to report the vibrations upon a higher plane of Existence. They do that only which they are made to do, and then they deceive us to a great extent.

It is now comparatively easy to understand how the vibrations of the infinitely finer grades of substance must entirely elude these physical organs, which are made and intended for physical vibrations only.

It is also comparatively easy to understand that a physically embodied man, by the aid of his physical sensory organs alone, cannot in any manner "sense" the presence of a disembodied spiritual man. The spiritual man is in being as truly as is the physical man, and yet he is neither physically tangible nor visible to the physical sensory organs. As with all substance invisible to the physical sensory organs alone, the vibratory action of the spiritual man cannot be detected by the physical sensory organs any more than can the vibratory action of electricity.

These facts of Existence, demonstrable to spiritual science, are already foreshadowed by modern physical science.

The claims of the older schools are substantiated by a series of lessons in science, written by Elisha Gray. Speaking of the physical sensory organs of wound and sight, this scientific authority says:

"While vibration ceases to affect our senses at 40, 000 beats per second, as sound, we find ourselves conscious again of periodic motion when it reaches 398 trillion tines per second. Then we hear with our eyes and see with our Ears, whichever you choose. The sensation in all cases is the effect of motion.

"The eye is the more perfectly developed, yet it is capable of only comparatively crude photography. The red ray canes to the eye with the lowest number of vibrations — four thousand billion. The eye cannot record anything with a less number of vibrations a second. The highest color is violet, with 764 trillion vibrations beyond which the eye cannot vibrate in sympathy with color. There are colors we cannot see. The Universe is filled with things that are invisible to the human eye and unknown to us.

"In the same way there are things that we cannot feel, and

odors that we cannot smell, and flavors that we cannot taste. For all we know, this world in which we live may also be the home of another race of beings, who pursue their course unknown to us, and perhaps we to them.

"It is the work of science to come to the aid of man's limited organism, and to lift a little the Veil of Mysteries."

Things spiritual cannot be described in our language of the physical world. For words -are deduced from things physical, hence words cannot fully express things spiritual, the significance, the bearings, the profundity of which transcend all that human thought can imagine and human skill can paint.

Chapter No. 7
Spiritual Substance (A)

Ancient Science had been destroyed, and all Europe was in utter darkness. The Papal Power reigned supreme. Then came the courageous Martin Luther. In 1317 he resolutely mailed to the door of "All Saints" church his Theses condemning the traffic of Indulgences by Romanism — thus striking that initial blow which started the decline of Papal Power, known in history under the deceptive and softer term "Reformation."

Encouraged by Luther's bold course, other man of courage began to defy Romanism, and from the ashes of these men a new Science was born.

The decline of Papal Power meant the decline of darkness. But it was a long and bitter struggle; and "heretics" were burnt right and left by the church. Between 1600 and 1670 in Spain alone, according to the record, the "Holy Roman Inquisition burnt alive 31,912 victims for the "Crime" of searching for Light.

"Curiously enough," writes Wall, "this mode of execution was introduced to avoid spilling human blood (*Sex Worship*, p. 339).

With the birth of a new science came the theory of Materialism, because these "heretical scientists" could not swallow the God theory of Romanism — and consequently they were Atheists. Materialism grew so fast in the next three centuries that Spiritualism became rank superstition. Yet, little knowing what they were doing, these physical scientists advanced to the very threshold of the Spiritual Realm, which they had claimed did not exist.

Science had said that the stem was indestructible. That theory is found to be false. More bewildering is the fact, that when Matter is reduced to its smallest invisible state, it dissolves as Matter and becomes Vibrating force, or Spiritual Substance, by science termed "energy."

Physical science was amazed with this startling discovery, and more amazed with the stupendous power of the Invisible Realm. Yet these scientists had seen trees uprooted as weeds by the terrific power of an invisible substance termed Wind.

In place of the scientific theory of solid, indestructible atoms, we now have protons, electrons, neutrons, etc. Instead of atoms being solid particles of matter, they are found to be composed of positive and negative units of Vibrating Force, and that Force, as we know it, is not "mechanical energy" but Spiritual Radiation.

The least secrets of ancient Science are slowly being rediscovered. The Spiritual Side of the Universe, the target of many scientific jokes, the alleged myth of the "superstitious heathens" of antiquity, is gradually appearing as a strange Reality. Scientific text-books will have to be rewritten.

We can begin to understand ancient scriptures; for they deal with the Spiritual World, the fourth Dimension, the Invisible Kingdom that was previously unknown to us.

Atomic dissolution appears as the ultimate source of certain force; and the quality of the force seems to depend on the character of the atomic elements prior to their dissolution. All matter has been invisible force, and all invisible force has been matter. Another example of the eternal cycle. Nothing begins and nothing ends.

When the Bible says "In the beginning," it means the

beginning of a certain kind of work.

The Masters taught that Cosmic Processes work in cycles. The visible from the invisible, and the visible to the invisible. We understand the invisible by the things made visible they said (Rom.1:20). This apparent mystery is no mystery at all when the fundamental principle is understood.

Water is invisible gas condensed. Ice is frozen water. Ice melts into water and water melts into vapor and returns to invisible substance.

All is one and one is all. We are part of every rock and bird and beast and hill. One with the things that prey on us, and one with what we kill. That is the law of Cosmic Relation.

There is only one world with two phases or aspects. Production (Creation) is a process of change. Lack of understanding causes us to be deceived by these changes.

Ice is not the opposite of water. Day is not the opposite of Night. Up is not the opposite of down. Matter is not the opposite of Spirit. Man is not the opposite of God. We are deceived by appearances and changes. All is one. Man is the Divine.

Ice and water are two aspects of the same thing. Spirit and Matter are two aspects of the same thing. God and Man are just as certainly and truly two aspects of the same thing. The law never changes. God is the invisible aspect of Spirit. Man is the visible aspect of Spirit. False teaching makes these statements hard for some to believe, yet they are statements of facts.

Production is the transition of the Invisible to the Visible, and from the visible back to the Invisible. That picture exhibits the work of the Law of Change and the Law of Cyclicity.

Henry Drummond (1851 - 1897) suddenly became famous by writing his *"Natural Law in the Spiritual World."* But half a million years before the Masters taught· the same doctrine in symbols and parables, the evidence of which appears in ancient scriptures.

Drummond advanced the theory that the "scientific principle of continuity extends from the physical world to the spiritual." The secrets of the Atom prove that he is right.

The Masters saw, in the Mind, the border-line between the two aspects of substance, and knew that every law of physical substance joins to its correlative law of spiritual substance.

Physical science cannot accept this philosophy without destroying its theory of Evolution; and Romanism cannot accept it without destroying its dogma of eternal damnation (Mark 16:16)

Ancient Science taught that the Cosmos is literally Universe, or a revolution around a center. Their doctrine of Unity, now confirmed by Spectrum Analysis and the Reign of law, was tersely summarized in the famous axiom of the Smaraqdine Tablet of Hermes: "That which is below is that which is above, and that which is above is that which is below."

Ancient Science taught what we are now discovering: Spirit is substance in its highest form of manifestation, and Matter is substance in its lowest form of manifestation. All substance existing between the two is the same, varying only in density from the finer to the grosser and vice versa. The Masters taught what modern science denies: The Living Organism is formed of condensed and consolidated spiritual substance, and animated by Spiritual Force. They regarded man as a dual being, existing in both the spiritual and material worlds, with the former eternal and the latter temporal. So they correctly said that man bears the image of the earthy and also the image of the heavenly. (1 Cor.

13:49).

Here we are again deceived by the state of dualism. We think there are two men as we think there are two worlds, one physical and one spiritual. There is only one man, and that one is the spiritual and eternal man, invisible to our physical senses.

Spiritual substance becomes material substance as the vibratory rate lessens. In this process the Spiritual manifests in different forms on different planes, assuming, in its transition, the Seven Principle Planes of Existence, listed by the Masters as (1) Divine-consciousness; (2) Cosmic Force and (Life); (3) Ether; (4) Fire (Electricity); (5) Air; (6) Water, and (7) Earth.

Occult science contends that Visible Objects are merely a reflection of Invisible Objects. The visible could not appear if the invisible did not exist; and the invisible is eternal whereas the visible is temporal.

The Masters said, "We look not at the things which are seen, but at the things which are not seen: for the things which are seen are temporal; but the things which are not seen are eternal."- - 2 Cor. 4:18. It is now known to be only a question of lowering the temperature and decreasing the vibrations that cause the different manifestations of Spirit on the different planes.

Physical science recognizes only the material world and the material man. Its dogma is to the effect that anything which cannot be materially demonstrated is unworthy of consideration and belief. It lives and labors in the physical realm of the five physical senses, which makes its knowledge necessarily very limited.

In addition to lowering the temperature, the vibratory rate is also reduced by inserting interferences into the path of invisible currents.

If we place a triangular piece of crystal, called a prism, in a ray of invisible light, thereby retarding its vibratory rate, visible effects appear in the form of the seven colors, each color passing at a different rate of vibration.

A certain voltage of electrical pressure produces heat, light motion, and may be harmless to man. A higher voltage is used for the execution of criminals. An immensely higher voltage, inducing current vibrations of thousands of millions per second, is harmless, the current being so swift that it speeds over the surface of the object without having time to penetrate the substance, hence no harm to him who receives this tremendous current practically unperceived.

Occult science shows that all manifestations in Nature, visible, physical, mental; spiritual, occur as transformations that are due to interferences, changes, projected into the rate of vibration of The imponderable Rays of the Universe.

The first interference, or the primary reduction of the vibratory rate, engenders the electro-magnetic lines of force. These, in turn, produce electric currents. The infinite combination of both, due to their limitless interconvertibility, projecting incessantly into the Cosmic Rays such an endless series of counter vibrations, that spiritual substance, gradually passing through the unperceivable state of essence, ultimately becomes visible in its transitions or changes, appearing in the tangible forms of liquids and solids. All of these phenomena are due to a lowering of the vibratory rate.

Water is a simple example of this transformative or so called creative process. It is a compound formed by the union of oxygen and hydrogen, two invisible gases. Actually, physical water per se does not exist. Water is only a name applied to a definite rate of vibration of visible substance, which rate occurs as a result of the union of two atoms of hydrogen and one atom of oxygen.

This union has the effect of lowering the vibrations and the phenomenon termed "water" appears. The phenomenon disappears as soon as the union of the atom is disrupted, which disruption increases the vibratory rate. It is all a question of vibration.

The union mentioned results from lowering the temperature, which reduces the vibrations. The union is dissolved by raising the temperature, which increases the vibrations, as when heated water transforms into steam.

This cosmic process guided the Masters directly into the department of the Invisible or Spiritual World. By applying the principle to all things, they discovered the Cosmic Law of Transformation, not Creation.

The cosmic process of transforming Spiritual Man into Physical Man is accomplished just as readily as that of transforming Spiritual Water into Physical Water.

The general principle is the same, but the process is more complicated, more difficult to explain and harder to understand.

Cosmic processes never change.

Chapter No. 8
Spiritual Substance (B)

In the final analysis, there is actually no such entity as physical man per se.

Physical man is merely a term given to a definite rate of vibration, set in motion by the union of various atoms — a process of transformation of spiritual substance to physical substance.

The phenomenon that appears, called Man, disappears, dissolves, dies, when the union and the equilibrium of the atoms is disturbed, deranged, thus disrupting the Cosmic Radiation that produces and sustains the phenomenon we know as Man.

Modern scientists have shown that as a visible entity, Man has "no existence in reality other than as waves, multitudinous and complicated centers, perhaps, in what we call the ether," writes Shelton. "Man is analogous in a sense," he continues, "to the sounds that issue from a piano when a chord is struck, or when a symphony orchestra sounds."

Physical man is a definite center of individual consciousness which appears as his own and which he thinks is his own, but which actually emanates from the Universal Center of Cosmic Consciousness.

For years, modern philosophers have been postulating a Cosmic Consciousness as a philosophical speculation for the future. Now that the Life Bearing Essence has been discovered, there is actual foundation for the theory.

Cosmic Consciousness has not yet been proven by physical methods, and it is still a subject for physical investigation. Occult science teaches that cosmic consciousness evolves in those who, by relaxing to the Life Bearing Essence, are able to relinquish most completely their sense of separateness from the Solar Center.

That was the secret the Masters taught to their disciples. It removes the barrier that man interposes in his ignorance by thinking that he is no part of the Spiritual world and only remotely related to the Universe. "For as he thinketh in his heart, so is he" (Pre. 23: 7).

Giovani Gentile wrote that there is a single imminent Ego that is the active consciousness or thinker in the brain. Physical science has now shown this to be a fact. The question that becomes paramount is the identity of the Ego. Is it the physical form or the Spiritual Essence? Most certainly the latter.

Occult science holds that the theorematic state of being conscious of being one with the Ego of the Essence, is Cosmic Consciousness.

It is an established fact that the material body has no consciousness per se. The consciousness it appears to have, is the Cosmic Consciousness unlimited, yet limited in the body by the body's limited capacity conscious expression.

Dr. Louis Berman in his *"Behind the Universe,"* holds that there is only one superior Personality in all of Existence; that in all time and space there is only one All-merging Consciousness.

No kind of continuous consciousness could exist until the brain was involved. There must be a union of our consciousness with all of life and all of the Universe. Berman contends that in telepathy there is already a union of the consciousness of two or more persons.

Only Cosmic Consciousness may be regarded as the objective reality of all things. That state of consciousness is the only state that establishes a bond between Physical Man and Spiritual man.

In 1874 Fisk said, "There must exist something which also existed before the Geneses of Intelligence, and which will prove to be the basis of all the truths of science."

Modern science admits that the brain is matter. But the Mind is not material nor a material product. There is and must be One Universal Mind. There is Universal Ego expressing consciousness in and through every human brain. The mind of man merely denotes cosmic consciousness in action.

The doctrine of Cosmic Consciousness is very old, and has always been recognized by occult science. New modern science has been constrained by its discoveries to admit that the doctrine is a fact.

Subjective and objective, mind and matter, are now seen to be one; and so it was taught by the Masters. Einstein shattered Newton's theory of gravity, but he postulated a greater mystery than Newton's in his theory of "curved space." We will never find truth by believing something first, and then searching for evidence to prove it.

A new discovery, like that of Cosmic Radiation, at once nullifies all former theories, based as they were on ignorance of what was then undiscovered.

The almost immeasurable small electrons of which the body is constituted are transformed by vibration into lines, and the lines intertwining among themselves, produce on our physical senses the impression of mass.

Mass is an illusion. There is as much space between the atoms of an iron bar, comparatively, as there is between the celestial planets.

What appears as solid matter is an illusion produced by the speed that appears to form the fine web of lines made by the traces of motion of the smallest material points.

Practically all the science we have developed so far is analytic. That is, we tear water apart and find it is composed of two invisible gases in certain proportions. Then we tear these two gases apart and discover how their nuclei are built up, and how many electrons revolve round the nuclei.

But there we, as finite beings, must stop. That is the borderline of the Spiritual World into which we, as conscious physical entities, cannot enter except by the power of Mind, which knows no limit. Our Mind we can flash into Space for millions of miles in a moment.

Physical science will discover in time that it is not the invention of finer instruments, but the improvement and freedom of the Mind of the investigators that will eventually solve the Mystery of Man.

Chapter No. 9
Spirit vs. Energy (A)

Modern science is founded on Materialism. It accounts for everything on the bases of physical matter and mechanical energy.

The theory of Materialism has been shattered by late discoveries. Now physical science must discard its text-books as obsolete and make a new start. The atom was said to be indestructible. Now it has been reduced to radiation, disappearing entirely as matter and becoming what science terms "energy."

Modern science is doing its utmost to "save face" and hide its errors by holding on to its term of "energy." The definition of Spirit and Energy discloses a vast difference between the two words.

SPIRIT — *Breath; breath of life; the principle of life; the soul; vital power. Immaterial intelligence; an intelligence conceived of separate from any physical organism. The intelligent, immaterial, and immortal part of man; the soul, as distinguished from the body which it occupies; as, the body without the spirit is dead.* — Webster's Unabridged Diet. 1915.

ENERGY — *Internal or internet power; the power of operating, whether exerted or not; strength or force producing the effect; the power of doing work.* — Ibid.

To an unprejudiced mind these definitions show that Spirit and Energy are entirely different things, bearing little relation to each other. The properties of Life and Intelligence are not attributed to Energy, but both are attributed to Spirit. Matter forms the visible aspect of the living organism. When matter is traced down to that point where it disappears as Matter and becomes a whirling center of force in the ether, only a materialist, an evolutionist, would apply the term "energy" to that mysterious specter that lies beyond the reach of the most powerful instruments of science. There is the border-line between the visible (temporal) and invisible (eternal).

If the vast, invisible, eternal part of the Universe is composed of and contains nothing more than "energy", then the visible, material part of the Universe should be empty and void; and Man must end and disappear forever when his body ceases its function. For if he is only consolidated "energy", he has no present Life and can have no Future life.

That is the precise and exact theory of modern science, of materialism, of evolutionism. That is the theory taught in the colleges and proclaimed in the text-books of physical science and medical art. These facts should be kept in mind by the student who is searching for Light.

If man represents only consolidated "energy'·, then that "energy", as consolidated matter, must have and possess all the properties and powers exercised by living man, including seeing, smelling, hearing, tasting, feeling, thinking, reasoning, etc. If that be the case, what becomes of these properties and powers when matter dissolves into "energy"? And how do they find their way into the body of a new-born present?

As explained in the *"World of Illusion,"* it is not "energy" that rises from the ashes of material substance. It is the Eternal Spirit of the Cosmos, in which inheres by law all the properties and powers exercised and expressed by all men in the Visible World of Nature, and which world is but a shadow of the vast Invisible World.

The Great Masters of antiquity called it Spirit, and they are supported in their choice of words by modern authors who define Spirit in dictionaries. That Spirit is not only the cause of "energy", but it is the source of all "energy". For "energy" is just one of its many properties.

Physical science would like to use the term Spirit, but it is forbidden by its own ethics to recognize anything under the definition of Spirit.

This is another instance of self-imposed limitation and ignorance made necessary to sustain the preconceived theories of Evolution, Matter, and Energy.

The definitions of Spirit and Energy conclusively show that one is so foreign to the other that the terms should never be used inter-changeably. To do so leads to error and confusion.

When the atom dissolves, the whirling centers of "energy" that appear in the ether are termed electrons. These are the building blocks of the Universe," says Millikan (Science & Now Giv. P. 118). No intelligent person would term Energy the building blocks of anything. It requires much more than "energy" to produce the Living World; and even physical science attributes to "energy" no other quality than that of activity or power.

Much more than power is required to build the Universe. The Power must be directed by Intelligence, the governing agent in every department of work. From this point of observation, the vast difference between Spirit and Energy becomes more obvious and much plainer. There are other differences, but for the present we have sufficient evidence to show that Living Organisms are much more than consolidated Energy.

He only who is too small and biased to admit that he is

wrong, would contend that undirected Energy, devoid of Intelligence, could do the vital work of building animal bodies and endowing them with Life and Intelligence.

Mighty man in the world of physical science have produced ponderous themes on the subjects of Force and Matter. Their plausible arguments and clever arrangements of words rule the scientific world. But new these text-books are largely obsolete. These men have held that Man is merely a material organism that functions as the result of a "series of chemical changes" occurring within the organism. That theory is proven to be erroneous.

Prof. J, S. Haldane, great astronomer says, *"materialism, once a plausible theory, is now the fatalistic creed of thousands (of physical scientists); but materialism is nothing better than a superstition, on the same level as a belief in witches and devils. The materialist theory (of physical science) is bankrupt" (Bible Mysteries Revealed,* p. 119).

Notice the effect when we copy that again and change only one word:

Evolutionism, once a plausible theory, is now the fatalistic creed of thousands of physical scientists; but evolutionism is nothing better than a superstition, on the same level as a belief in witches and devils. The evolutionist theory of physical science is bankrupt.

O. A. Wall, M.D., Ph.G., Ph. makes an interesting declaration on the subject of Evolution. He writes:

"I graduated as a physician from Bellevue Medical College in the same year that Darwin published his work on the *Descent of Man*. The 'Conflict between Science and Religion' that ensued, was fought out and the truth of the theory of Evolution was established within the period of my professional career. And with this victory of human thought, many superstitions faded away "(*Sex Worship*, 1922, p. 37).

With the victory of modem science in reducing the atom to invisible "energy," these "superstitions" bobbed right back again into human thought. Evolutionism and Materialism must stand together or fall together. For the former is founded on the latter. If the "Materialist theory is bankrupt" so is the "evolutionist theory."

Prof. Ludwig Buchner, M.D., strong protagonist of Materialism and Evolutionism, wrote:

"No force without matter, no matter without force. One is no more possible and no more imaginable by itself than the other. Separated from each other, each becomes an empty abstraction or idea, which is useful only in showing two sides or manifestations of the same existence, the nature of which, in itself, is unknown to us. Force and matter are fundamentally the same thing, contemplated from different standpoints" (Force & Matter).

Buchner is right in his conclusion, but his conclusion left him in darkness. He admitted that the nature of the object and premise on which his conclusion rested, was "in itself unknown to us."

That "unknown" property was known to the masters, and has now been discovered by modem science. But science is bound by its ethics not to give a true, correct and definite description and recognition of what it has found.

Chapter No. 10
Spirit Vs. Energy (B)

We have previously quoted from that exceptional work, produced by the combined labor of six leading scientists, titled *"Marvels & Mysteries of Science."* On p. 409 thereof appears this statement:

"It was once thought that living things possessed energy which was lacking in the inanimate, but with a clearer understanding of matter, it has become apparent that Matter never exists free from energy. In fact, Matter may be nothing more than a manifestation of energy itself. "

It would be the most stupendous miracle ever presented for human contemplation if we were required to imagine that the Cosmos and all its parts are the product of blind, undirected Energy, which the dictionary defines as only a power capable of moving against resistance.

For the products constructed of whirling electrons, termed "the building blocks of the Universe", exhibit in their conduct a high degree of Intelligence, even to the point of infinity.

Millikan was a scientist, yet he disregarded the ethics of his profession by stating that Matter is Spirit condensed into visibility, much the same as invisible vapor is condensed into ice.

According to this declaration, Matter is the visible aspect, not of blind and undirected Energy, but of Spirit directed by Intelligence.

The Masters had this subject in mind when they carved the inscription on the ancient pyramid of Sais, which reads, *"I am all that is, that was, and that will be. No Mortal man has, yet raised my veil."*

To that statement of the Masters, F. J. Pisko replies, "Modern science has removed the veil and discovered that force and matter were, are, and will be.

But that boastful reply is already obsolete. Pisko's Force and Matter have vanished into the Spiritual World as a whirling vortex in the ether. And the veil of Isis has not yet been raised.

Electronics research has brought man to the edge of the invisible mysteries. He has reached for the stars and discovered the Electronic Era, where the visible melts into the invisible.

Alessandro Volta discovered the electric current. It is only in the last half century that physical science has learned much about electricity.

It is almost half a century since Marconi proved to an astonished science that messages could be transmitted to distant points without wires.

Tonight a sailor in the distant Pacific talks by radio with his mother in the USA. A band plays in New York City, and five thousand miles away people dance to the music. Modern science had declared that space is empty and void.

In the air we breathe are wonders no man can explain with every breath we are linked with our Divine Origin more closely than we realize. The mystery of Life itself may be learned by studying the Breath of Life breathing itself within us.

The different qualities that distinguish the various types of Matter are merely the difference in the number and arrangement of the protons and electrons composing the atom of these various types. Man is again entering the Atomic Age in which were the Masters who carved out of solid rock, with atomic power, the amazing temples of the world. He has discovered that Substance, in the form of Spirit, fills the space of the Universe which modern science had declared was empty and void. The atom is the smallest unit of matter known. Almost a million of them could set side by side on the point of a sharp needle.

Atoms are globular systems in which electrons, protons, neutrons, etc., revolve with lightning speed round their common center of attraction, like the planets and the sun of our solar system, They are held in their orbits and regulated as to the combinations they form by the field of electro-magnetic force generated by their motions.

It is startling to think of what occurs in the human body, composed of trillions of cells, and each cell composed of atoms, and each atom a miniature solar system vibrating with vital force that is inherent in spiritual substance.

It is possible to match the stupidity of a system that contends such a body is built, sustained and energized by food arid drink. Were that contention true, then the earth, moon, stars and suns would have to be supplied with food and water or perish.

An atom of Uranium has 92 "planets," and each planet is, in size to an atom, as a grain of fine sand is to a regular football. It would take 500 trillion of them to fill the bulk space in the atom, and each cell of the human body is composed of trillions of atoms. These "planets revolve planet-like with great speed in an atom, around a nucleus composed of protons and ·neutrons. Electrons (planets) carry a negative electrical charge. Protons (also planets) have a positive charge. Neutrons (also planets) have no charge.

Each atom has as many electrons as protons, their respective electrical charges neutralizing each other and keeping the tiny system in perfect equilibrium.

Most of the atom appears as space, as most of our solar system appears as space. A cubic inch of water weighs about half an ounce. A cubic inch of solid nuclear matter would weigh more than a billion tons. The practically unlimited power of polar attraction holds together the particles that constitute the nucleus.

The materialist says that the atom is held together by tremendous electric voltage. In splitting the atom, called fission, these voltages are released in the form of force. In the atomic bomb, the atoms of Uranium were broken in two — liberating the astounding power of 200,000,000 electron volts per atom

It is said that electricity is electrons in transit. That gives us some conception of the tremendous force contained in atoms. The laboratory of be human body is so constituted as to utilize that atomic power; and that is the power, under proper control, which performs all the various functions of the living organism.

The absurd theory of modern science that vital force, nerve force, brain force, and body function are the product and result of food and drink is completely shattered.

As the Universe is the Microcosm, so Man is the Microcosm. By discovering the constitution of Man, we also discover the constitution of the Universe. We search, with giant telescopes, in the far reaches of the sky for cosmic secrets, and miss them; yet they may be discovered in the atoms at our feet or in our body.

Atoms are miniature solar systems. When we realize that fact, we shall know the secrets of the Universe.

Chapter No. 11
The Cosmic Pattern

Recent research in atomic physics and in psychic mysteries has shown the existence of worlds composed of substances and forces with rates of vibration much too high for our five-sense powers to register.

The external phenomena which our five senses contact, are but the materialized expressions of cosmic causes generated in the super physical worlds, which can be contacted only by our psychic (sixth) and spiritual (seventh) sense powers. All ancient scriptures deal largely with these super-physical worlds, and their relation to the material world in which physical man dwells.

Under the law that something comes not from nothing, then archetype or ideals of all manifested forms must have pre-existence in the super-physical realms as a pattern-ideal, etheric double or model, as explained in our work *"Pre-Existence of Man,"* or there would be nothing to direct cosmic forces in the production of symmetrical and definitely organized forms.

This doctrine of the pre-existence of all things before their physical manifestation, is illustrated in many biblical passages, and is mentioned by Littlefield, who said: *"All visible form; have their counterpart in the invisible world"* (P. 180).

Lakhovsky supported this doctrine. He wrote: *"Under the law of cosmic radiation, physical man appears as the materialization of his spiritual duplicate. His visible form is a replica of his invisible frame"* (*Secret of Life*).

The Bible says *"Every plant of the field (was in the air) before it was in the earth,"* and *"every herb (was in the air) before it grew"* **(Gen. 2:5).**

The pre-existence of man was purposely omitted here, being held up and added later to the fable of the gospel Jesus to make him appear greater:

"Verily, verily, I (Man) **say 'unto you, · Before Abraham was, I** (Man) Am".

Before material man was visible on the earth, he was invisible in the Spiritual Realm. This ancient doctrine is the basis of all great religions of the ancient world, and is implicit in most philosophies. All material formations change, and anything that changes is of the realm of the temporal and transitory, and not of the permanent and eternal.

Eternal Reality exists only in the super-physical, unchanging realms, where the prototypes or pattern-ideals exist. The fact that pre-existing etheric patterns of all material forms are invisible, is not evidence that such are only imaginary, or are only rental concepts, and have no actual existence. *'The air we breathe, odors, colorless gases, and atoms, are all of them invisible, yet they all actually exist and affect us and our lives.*

A field or force, such as surrounds the ends of a magnet, has both form and extension, but it is invisible to us. We must not forget that substance is also atomic, etheric, and radionics, and that a large part of the universe is invisible to our five senses and unknown to us.

The renowned naturalist Louis Agassiz correctly said, "Nature is the work of Intelligence carried out according to plan, therefore is premeditated, n and that "All things have their origin in Spirit."

'The term "premeditated" is misleading. It causes the exoteric to believe that the church God, man-like, did some thinking and designing before making the visible world and all things therein, including man, that may have been the viewpoint of Agassiz.

The involution of the pattern must have preceded its evolution in substance, or there would be no pattern to unfold into an organized form.

As we said in *"Pre-Existence of Man,"* it logically follows that as man is the most highly evolved form in all visible existence, he must also exist antecedently as the highest super-physical archetype or pattern which Cosmic forces unfold and materialize into physical man in the physical realm. As man is the highest in the physical world, he must also be the highest in the super-physical world. As man is the God of all the earth, he must also be the God of all the heavens.

Man is much more than a physical body. The Real Self is a Spiritual Entity, manifesting temporarily thru a physical body in the visible world. But existing eternally in the invisible world.

As there is but one basic Law of Transformation, it follows that all expressions on the physical plane emanate from the super-physical world, and, in turn, pass on from the visible back to the invisible. That is the Cosmic Cycle. *Nothing that is, ever comes to an end.*

Man's Faulty Knowledge

Man's five special sense organs give him some information of the universe, and of himself, but leave him ignorance of a larger part of it, and deceive him as to the most of that which they give him.

Our eyes register only a few rays of light and disclose only a small part of the horizon. Our ears fail us when vibratory waves are too short or too long.

If we were to reason according to the evidence our five sense organs furnish us, we would have a very crude idea of the world, and a very false one. Yet that is the condition in which the masses live, along with that deceptive system termed material science, and a religious system based on fraud.

For sixteen hundred years, since the destruction of the Ancient Wisdom in the fourth century, humanity has been obliged to rely solely upon these means for knowledge. Hence, not only is that knowledge faulty, meager, and misleading, as we have discovered, but men have believed that beyond that the five senses reveal, there was nothing.

That is the state in which lived the scientists of the 17th, 18th, and 19th, and early part of the 20th centuries, when they invented their theory of evolution.

Their errors are being corrected in all departments of learning, but slowly, because these scientists are trying hard to hide their errors from the eyes of the world. These scientists have held that Matter is the primary and sole reality, consisting of infinitely fine particles which clash and cohere into molecules and larger lumps, and finally are refined into higher grades of organization in the brain.

Our knowledge, affections, will, life and our very Soul, are only the effects of the activities of atom; and chemical changes.

Behaviorism, the latest form of materialism, denies that man has any consciousness.

Thinking consists only of certain twitching's of the muscles in the throat, and our feelings, in the elegant language of Behaviorism, are only "the squirming of the guts."

Think of that when you next read about "*The March of*

Science."

Chapter No. 12
Constitution Of Man

Modem science has been constrained by its recent discoveries to admit that there is one imminent Ego which appears as the Active Consciousness of the Thinker in and through the human Brain. In his book *Thinking & Destiny*, Harold W. Percival calls it the Thinker and the Doer.

EGO — Literally, the "I"; the Real Self that sees, smells, hears, feels, thinks, reasons, wills and acts, as distinguished from its attributes, from the bodily organization, and from every other object or thought; the subject as distinguished from everything objective. — Dictionary.

According to the dictionary, Spirit and Ego may be considered the sane entity. The Spirit is said to be "the intelligent, immaterial and immortal part of man," while the Ego is termed the "I" that does all which man thinks he does of himself.

'The inner and outer world are me. The visible and invisible worlds are one. Spirit and Ego are one. Our Life is one Life; and that all is the manifestation of — WHAT? Who has the answer? The church does not.

Man is not only part of the Universe, but an important part. He is the highest organized Entity known. In his Constitution he illustrates all the Principles of the Universe.

It appears that (1) Force performs, (2) Intelligence directs, and (3) Matter appears as if by magic in definite forms, from the invisible world. The mystery would vanish if the Principle were understood.

The Ego remains invisible within the living organism, yet it is the source and cause of the body's formation, animation, and function. Ego is neither function, process, nor product, but the cause of them all.

Vitality in the stomach digests all kinds of non-living flesh, but the stomach does not digest itself, nor can it digest a living body, as a reptile, that may have found its way therein. For Vitality is superior to chemistry.

In man, Ego appears as Mind; and Mind is King, not subject; the Master, not the servant. Ego is in, above, and behind all, with the body as its Temple in which it dwells and through which it works.

The work man performs, as sawing wood or shoveling coal, is an example of what science terms "energy." But "energy" rises from Ego in action. "Energy", the product of Ego in action, may do physical work, but only Vital Force can do vital work. That is the great difference between Spirit and Energy, but a difference not recognized by science.

Construction and repair of the body are vital processes, performed by Vital Force. They need no aid from doctors, drugs, vaccines and serums.

To carry on the functions of living, there are and must be involved both vital and physical processes, — the former to direct and control, and the latter to perform and serve.

Science ignores the vital and sees only the work of physical and chemical processes. According to science, intelligence to direct and control is superfluous and unnecessary.

Vitality appears as the Ego in action. It appears as Infinite Power, illustrating an Intelligence that seizes upon and employs for its processes all things that may be of service to it. It is the repairing as well as the producing power.

Recovery from illness is repair work, not healing work. The only power that can repair the body is the power that produces it.

The mechanism of the living organism is too delicate, too intricate, too complex, and too little understood to admit of repair by any agency other than the Producing Power.

The process of repair is the process of production, performed by the same power that brought the body into being. That power is never delegated to man, nor group of men. Nor to medical institutions.

The term "healing" is erroneous. It is all repair work; and the power of repair is the Power of Life that performs all body functions.

The mechanic does not "heal" a damaged car; he repairs it. But doctors cannot repair the body's derangements; regardless of their claim. No scientist can make a drop of blood, nor a piece. of bone.

As only Life can produce the body, only Life can repair the body.

If so-called physical and chemical "energy" could be transformed into Vital Force, as claimed by modern science, the length of man's life would be largely in his own hands,

The irony of it all is, that the scientists who make such claims are noted chiefly for their short life-span.

Food and drink being inferior to Life, cannot produce Life Vital Processes, physical science to the contrary.

If these substances could produce Life, then the USA should be a Land of exceptional longevity, with giants more than a thousand years old.

Why should man ever die with plenty of food and drink to be

had?

Chapter No. 13
Spiritual Contact

J. S. Haldane, noted astronomer said, "Materialism, once a plausible theory, is not the fatalistic creed of thousands (of physical scientists), but Materialism is nothing better than a superstition, on the same level as a belief in witches and devils. The Materialist Theory of bankrupt."

The materialistic theories of Bacon and Descartes appear to have laid the foundation of modern science. With the explosion of these theories, science is left empty handed and forced to make a new start.

Descartes regarded Extension and Matter as practically synonymous terms: "Give me Extension and motion, and I will construct the world."

In this aphorism the difference between his views and Bacon's is epitomized, whereas the latter clearly realized the need of empirical data, Descartes greatly over-estimated the possibilities of deduction.

Material science, newly embarked on a long course of triumphs in its own chosen domain, became more and more enamored of the materialistic hypothesis that everything happens and can be explained by mechanical and therefore measurable causes.

It has taken three centuries of materialism to test this one sided Cartesian metaphor, in which Nature is regarded as a machine, and to explode the fallacy. And so three centuries of materialism have come to a sad end. Science finds embarrassment in the fact that its mechanical theory of the Universe is falling apart. Its errors are beginning to be recognized in quarters where, until yesterday so to speak, the assumption that Nature and Man were nothing more than accidentally assembled machines was the root-axiom of scientific enlightenment.

When apparently solid matter dissolves and disappears, we must pursue it in the spiritual world with the mind, as the Masters did. (Rom. 1: 20). They investigated the Psychic Phenomena of Life, and with them the modus operandi of Spiritual Force was the subject of deep study for thousands of years.

Had Roman Catholicism and modern science not joined forces in stigmatizing the Ancient Masters as "heathenish pagans" who dumbly worshipped idols and false gods, and then carefully destroyed their scriptures to hide the actual facts, the world would today have a Science of Religion and a Science of Man instead of a Crucified God and a Theory of Evolution.

These idols and false gods were images used by the Masters to teach the neophyte the Mysteries of Life, and were only symbols of Cosmic Principles and Cosmic Processes.

Romanism adopted these same symbols and transformed them into gods and angels, men and devils, satan and purgatory, hell and heaven, and then developed the worse system of idolatry the world has ever known. That system is tottering to its final fall.

When science exploded its own theory that atoms were the ultimate of matter, one scientist then said, "Matter is nothing but condensed electricity."

It is well at this point to take the same step in another direction, and declare that so-called disease is only the symptoms of internal poisoning.

From the Masters we can learn much about the operation of Cosmic Forces; about the real purposes of the different parts of the brain and the mysterious chakras or spiritual nerve centers, of which the glands are only the external symbols; about the spiritual channels and magnetic currents that flew through the body; about the strange Serpentine Fire generated in the sacral plexus at the base of the spine.

As these spiritual centers of the body are not visible, not dissectible, nor measurable with material instruments, the theory of their existence is scornfully rejected by medical art.

The fact that man-made instruments cannot detect these subtle centers on the physical plane means nothing, as we have shown in *The Mysterious Sphinx* and *The Magic Wand*.

Man's subconscious mind rules his body's involuntary functions. This is the secret link that connects Conscious Man with Cosmic Consciousness, as explained in our work *"Kingdom of Heaven."*

Spiritual Contact is the term applied to this connection. It is a contact actually capable of physical demonstration, but concerning which science, remains silent.

Let us cite an illustration: The eye of the unconscious man cannot see; his ear cannot hear. What is the reason? Spiritual. Contact is absent, as we have sham in "Kingdom of Heaven,

The existence of the spiritual forces of occult physiology were accepted as facts by the Masters, just as modem science is forced to accept as a fact the existence of Mind, Nerve, Force, etc.

The present and existence of spiritual forces must be recognized by their fruits (Mat. 7: 18)

So these forces of living bodies prove their existence in the results obtained by the Masters and occult students who have studied them.

Prof. Buchner, one of these material scientists, says that Matter, in the form of Man, possesses mind, sensation and consciousness, which result from a 'mode of motion" arising from the interaction of physical forces.

How can a scientist be so blind? So dumb? Who wants to follow him? That is the brand of nonsense the world accepts today as science; and the world remains in darkness. Those who question or attack that nonsense are silenced and liquidated by the "powers that be."

When matter melts and disappears, and then re-appears again, reason informs us that this is the work of an invisible cause.

Buchner says, 'The laws by which nature works and acts are the natural and necessary expressions of the interaction of all physical forces from which arise certain laws."

But Nature does not work and act. Nature is a name applied to the visible phenomena resulting from the work and action of an unseen force. Nature is the product. An invisible cause does the work, and Nature is the effect.

The fragments of the philosophies that we have of the Ancient Masters, show that their whole work dealt with Man and Life, and not with gods, saviors and heaven. That twist was put into the ancient writings by the church fathers when they prepared their Bible to serve the church, not the people.

The Masters discovered that Cosmic Principle presents dual but equilibriums properties: positive and negative, active and passive, initiative and receptive, — also called male and female.

They found that the proper relation and balance between

these two Principles govern the transformation, production, development, decline and disintegration of all living things, as we have explained in *The Mysterious Sphinx* and *The Magic Wand*.

The cosmic process of transforming solarized man into physical man. Illusion. The dual aspect. The sense of separateness. The identity of the ego. The secret of the atom. Doctrine of numbers.